More Than Meat
and Raiment

More Than Meat and Raiment

Poems

Angela Jackson

TRIQUARTERLY BOOKS / NORTHWESTERN UNIVERSITY PRESS

EVANSTON, ILLINOIS

TriQuarterly Books
Northwestern University Press
www.nupress.northwestern.edu

"Wishbone Wish" is based on a Hausa tale, "The City Where Men Are Mended," one version of which can be found in the anthology *African Myths and Tales*, edited by Susan Feldmann (New York: Dell, 1963), 232–36.

Printed in the United States of America
10 9 8 7 6 5 4 3 2 1

Library of Congress Cataloging-in-Publication Data

Names: Jackson, Angela, 1951– author.
Title: More than meat and rainment : poems / Angela Jackson.
Description: Evanston : TriQuarterly Books/Northwestern University Press, 2022.
Identifiers: LCCN 2021042678 | ISBN 9780810144569 (paperback) |
    ISBN 9780810144576 (ebook)
Classification: LCC PS3560.A179 M67 2022 | DDC 811/.54—dc23
LC record available at https://lccn.loc.gov/2021042678

Is not life more than food? Is not the body more valuable than cloth?

—Matthew 6:25 (*New American Bible*)

CONTENTS

II. Wishbone Wish

III. Soul World

ACKNOWLEDGMENTS

Several of these poems appeared in *TriQuarterly* online, *Tribes*, *Poetry* magazine, *The Eloquent Poem*, *Bennington Review*, *Revise the Psalm*, and *Another Chicago Magazine*. My gratitude to the editors.

My gratitude also to Major Jackson, Amy Gerstler, Timothy Liu, and Ed Ochester, Sven Birkerts and Victoria Clausi and the Bennington Writing Seminars.

Truly to Imani Elizabeth Jackson, Johnetta Awthentik Anderson, and avery r. young, who keep me young and sometimes wiser.

Finally, a debt of gratitude to Ms. JoAnna Johnson for her faithful preparation of these poems in manuscript.

To Parneshia Jones, who opens doors wide and inviting. To Anne Gendler, for precise understanding and clarity.

To Krista Franklin for her miraculous artwork, and to Morgan Krehbiel, who set it off beautifully on the cover.

Thank you to all of these and to family and true friends steadfast.

Thanks and praise.

I. Hero-House

An African American Saga of Drylongso in the Great Migration

*For my nieces and
great-nieces,
my nephews and
great-nephews
For the Black Family*

The Guide

for Debra Anne Jackson, 1958–2008

We caught fireflies with our bare hands,
Holding them in cupped palms as if in prayer.
Then we jailed them in glass jars and watched
Them signal to us distress or innocent bliss.

Sometimes we tore their lights from them
And pinned the shimmer to our earlobes
In adornment. We were children of summer.

Grown older, past many seasons, in another region
Of the country, in the company of poets
I trudged toward my rooms as evening
Began to hint descent and fireflies to circle,
Blinking and moving away, coming and going.

Little sister, I had it wrong, and thought
Your soul a firefly, diminutive and incandescent,
But that dusk a wise woman who studies
The ways of the First People told me they say
The firefly guides souls to the other side.

Two Peoples say the same. Oh, sister.
Two nights before you died, a firefly lit
The dark of our living room.
The entire room glowed. So tiny a being
Casting such a big, sweet light.

We had never seen a firefly so brave to arrive inside.
The light so bright in the darkness to guide you
To the other side. There must be a river somewhere.

I know on this side of the deep River of Life and Death,
Weeping, grief and relief at once, how you made it there,
The other side, how you made it.

And that early evening in another region I went so blind
From tears, my love for you the only light I could see
Where fireflies circled, just beyond my reach.

Heat Wave

In this *Negro Story*
a baby will sleep
on a car ride
from one life
the rocking sway
the push out
to *Bronze Thrills* and heating bills
through sunlight
and black night high-
ways following the spraying beams
of headlights

All around—
waves, deep amber people.
deeper *Tan*, deep *Ebony*, *Jet* black, mixed waves
as wild rice, tobacco, heat waves blinding
bright as cotton, clothes
swinging on a line, like any colored bodies.

Palms turning
flat fans
newspapers, *Chicago Defender* against
the heat, waves
of people, waving
the leave-taking song,
Every good-bye ain't
gone.

On the way
to *Bright Lights, Big City*
Bright Lights, Big City,
a *Negro Digest*

a *Black World* soon.

Higher Ground

He came home from the service
and didn't want to swing from wood or serve
crackers or Jim Crow.
He scouted North: job, house.
                    He had some nerve.
Sent for us to come through the front door.

Boxes strapped to the roof
of the car, children crammed inside
like matches in a book,
ready to set the City on fire.

Blues, a burning fuse, up Highway 61.
Up we spun, bright spark, women, men, girls, boys,
through Tennessee, Arkansas,
                    through long Illinois.

Cairo (not Egyptland, but white
            Karo syrup) not sweet,
Mean as any
Mississippi Goddam.

He Was a Trained Carpenter

See this painting—
Boy Breaking Glass.
How about a man who was used to kickin ass?
The White City sucked in its breath.

Mama says—"He was a carpenter.
There was a storefront he bought.
He broke all that glass
and made two apartments.
One in front and one in back.
He went to school down south for that."

(I am tempted to ask—
"What did he do with all
that glass? How exactly
did he break it? Chisel it out?
Or hammer it like John Henry?")

He stepped over a threshold.
Built a new city around us.

A Country Girl

31. A country girl. She came to the City
to the house, second floor,
Mississippi at her back, a baby girl in the ground,
holy then with grief and memory.
The City so big, she thought, the buildings loomed.
In Mississippi in elementary school
she'd learned about the Mecca, the Rosenwald Building.
So many Negroes in one space, imagine the heat
that much Black drew. She laughed easily. She wanted to be
a part of progress. I imagine her. "Good goodness of life!"
Five children already, spotless, shiny like new pennies
to meet the City. I was her lap baby.
She came to that house and trembled at the bigness
of the City, following up behind her husband.
But it was her dream too, to spread out and up
like Chicago. They piled into the second floor,
two families, her and a sister-in-law, and she determined they
would make it. "The windows so long
and wide! You can see across the street,
the streetcar line." She would take her children,
ride the streetcar to the Lincoln Park Zoo, then
come back on the streetcar and jump off like acrobats.
One time they jumped off and left Prentiss behind, he kept going
and Sonny, her long-legged elder son, had to race
the streetcar down and bring Prentiss home to her
in front of that house where she waited with her arms akimbo,
torn between laughing and crying. She wasn't about to lose
another child. Not to this city. Not this country girl.

Beside the House

Carnations
on the south side
of the house, hugging
and sprawling red.

I never would have thought
my father would have thought
of such
lovely touches.
Soft, tight, swirling petal-cups
holding all that blood-color,

A little low fence around it.

The Garden

In the backyard—
The monkey cigar tree
Prosperous as a banker.

Tree of heaven
Stretching halfway there.

Through the alley
Behind the convent,
Crabapple, with bite-sized fruit,
Tart, impudent like us,
Sweet blackberries breaking
On the sidewalk.

These grew on their own.
Willingly,
The rest my father planted.
Whatever would rise—
Willingly.
Willfully.
Greens, beans, okra, peppers,
Eggplant, onions, tomatoes,
My mother put away
Like perfect specimens
In shining mason jars.

Tenants

Cardinal Alex Houston Reneau.
A son's name for ecclesiastical
Authority.

       Those kind of people
Bowed to few. Had a little.

They came from Honduras.
Lived on the first floor
Back. Then the father had more pride
Than my father.
He would not take orders
From a boss.

In separate years
The Hamptons, an expensive resort name
For poor people, mystery-sick. First floor,
Front, lived and died, one by one.
Fate plucked them from their mother,
Father.

Adair, my age-mate,
Loved to play,
Could not say a clear word.
Wobbled in the doorway

The baby boy began in hope,
Plump as a cantaloupe. Withered.
What was his name?

Only Jack remained.
Played guitar. Sang
A song to my sisters.

I wonder how he died.
Or tried to stay
Past the number
Of his days.

Madaddy and the Honduran Man

The Honduran man—
those staircase children
he climbed
with a heavy tread.

The woman a backdrop,
a prop,
who managed
to go unnoticed.

Our house
at last
was beneath him.
My father rejoiced—
or did he just put him
out?

Perhaps
they parted company
like the Red Sea
we children all ran through
to be free

of men with far-dreams,
the pride of lions,
and fists like pistons.

Years after
Madaddy planted gardens.
We saw the warm
sun in his eyes.

What did the Honduran man
plant?
Was he ever so tender
with the work of his hands?

If he ever worked.
That was my father's grudge
against him.

A man spose to be
doin' something with
his hands.

A man spose to be
makin' a way
outta no way
ev'y day,
but Sunday.

Did that man Honduran
ever go to church?
My father visited Jesus
on special occasions.

Took off his hat.
In God's house he was
a tenant

who paid his rent
with the work of his hands.

His soul a bruised
and shining coin

Offering.

Overnight

Summer nights when the heat did not recede
From steel mills, or crowded factories,
Dark people staggered out of tenements and houses,
Children in tow, in arms.
They moved down the avenue, slow and quick,
Sweat on their skin like Kool-Aid,
                          Toil and tears.

At that lean park between streets,
They fanned out blankets, and dropped pillows on the soft grass,
Then they put children down and threw their arms wide

To try to catch
A wandering breeze, the only thing free.

Summer and the City

(Chicago then, in memory of Robert Hayden and his memory)

Summer nights cool came down
Blotting heat like a kiss for colored children.
Heat surged
As we danced jagged up and down the street
Played hide-and-seek:
Last night, night before
Twenty-four robbers
At my door
I got up
Let 'em in
Hit 'em in the head
With a rollin pin
All hid? Among the leaves
Of church hedges
We smelled
Something slow and splendid
In our sweat.

Our fathers we knew worked good
Jobs that required muscle.
Our mothers in day work
Used elbow grease and unwritten receipts
For smothered chicken and gravy
Caused white women to envy and delight.

Outside mothers waited for aid checks
And the long-gone man; large women
On folding chairs
Ate chunks of Argo starch.

Lean days, sugar sandwiches,
Ketchup, or mayonnaise.
Missing meat a vague notion.
Love, manna.

Twilight blessed the blocks,
Poured from a dark man's mouth
like a spout of Joe Louis milk,
Our champion toast.

Heralding the greatest arrival,
However long the getting there,
Slow rocking grandmothers
Spit out words into small cans
Held in their hands.

Their eyes trained on us
From Deep South porches
We never left behind

Never left us

Even after Exodus.

Mouths wide open, we drank
The evening's pleasure.
Men, women who loved us more
Than what we could have known.
We were their quick, flashing hope
                                    treasures
The memory of us
Their milk.   Their honey.

Homemade Rolls

for Leslie Jackson

Aromas rose through wide rooms.
Origin of all warm and sufficient
Was the kitchen
Where she ruled
With a beneficent hand.
She laid the dough on the table
And seduced it with able
Fingers,
Tossing a flurry of flour
Like dry snow over a thick sheet
Of malleable dough.
Whatever to be
She made it
In that kitchen
Where the windows
Shone glassy-eyed like sovereign saints.
Nothing could go wrong
In a world
Where rolls rose
Soundlessly
On the ledge of the stove,
Where she placed them
At the moment of their height,
Then drew them out,
Brown almost as we were,
But not tough,
Soft, falling apart
So unlike us
And our delectable way of life.

Novenas

Tuesday evenings
The house opens its mouth.
She walks out, head-scarved,
Starved to find a way.
On her mind
Never more than she
Can carry.

        —Pray Ethel will have children
        Four; Then
        Pray Ethel will have
        No more.

St. Anne, the crossroads
Of hope and grinding stone. Rosary voices soft, fluttering
Women, Our Lady of Perpetual Help.
        Prayer lifts. Repairs all rifts.
The women rise.
Stroll homeward.
Her friend, Dollye, heat packed in her purse,
Removed her lace caplet, bareheaded, brave.
Her mouth tough.
Our mama she lingers before the house.
Its open eyes
Welcoming at dusk.
Laughing at shadows unfettered
Daughters, Our Lady of Perpetual Help.

The house raises up.

Bills

Dollar bills do not fly over distances
        like bright green birds
        perched momentarily
        to mimic a song.

Dollars float down
        like leaves
        not far from trees.

My father squeezed dollar bills
in a wallet thick with IDs and papers
to give the appearance of wealth,

a flock of green birds rustling inside
to get out for some extravagance
(Baldwin's ice cream for each of us!),

but inside were dry leaves
pressed together cramped as the pages
of the Bible he did not need to read
to pray with his tight fists.

Christmas Eves

Christmas Eve overflowed when
my father opened his hands
and the jubilee began.
He brought forth baskets of apples
and oranges like domesticated suns.
He lay manifold hands of bananas on the table.
Every nut we knew cracked like policemen cracked heads—
sweet pecans, walnuts, hazelnuts, rough Brazilian
nuts—bought by the bushel.
A turkey to roast big as a bull.
Tender no matter pounds.
In mid-night after midnight mass
the man who brought in the tall fir tree
went on school-time missions with
our mother to bring back Sorry, Monopoly,
Scrabble each year and Black or white dolls
and tiny plastic soldiers
celebrated
a baby born with nothing
but poor people to love him.

She was always Mary
of the smiling virgin delivery,
and he was Joseph
and three wise men, traveling,
following a generous star
through a year of caution
and plotting pennies,
benevolent secrecy.

Club DeLisa

In spring years he danced at DeLisa
Saturday nights on State Street, then came
home to entertain her with
legends of his legs so limber
and true they outwitted
smoke threading through sleek sepia
bodies releasing memories
of captivity and defeat.
Wide-eyed, she listened and laughed
and nursed a new baby. Knowing
with his ticket for safekeeping.
She was his cigarette girl
with tray in front, in back
her butt and legs with sexy straight seams.

She'd show him something, one of these
smoky Saturday evenings.

Not Your Government Name

Yuk Yuk, DoFunny,
Mr. Git., Leave-Ma-Be.

Sonny Man,
Peaches, Dolly.
That's me.

The names we hid inside.
The names inside we shine.

Coota, Bay Bay,
BaySuh, BabyDo,
Buddy, Sweet,
Tumpy, Teedle-Lump,
TooDoo.

Names like clean clothes
Hung on a line

Dancing in bright wind
and noon-shine.

Hot Fun in the Summertime

Three in college at once!
Our parties in summer brought out
the best of us
citywide.

The windows opened to a breeze
we found
to cool our sweat
in the hothouse
where Afros bloomed.
We were the rage.

We danced vocabulary of intelligent toughness
One-fifty-one rum punch
not for punks or babies
who hung around the knees of the dining room table,
dancing with the chaperones.
Mama showed us how to make
a feast for dreamers and rappers
when rapping and the rap were love offerings
or wise, smooth parts of speech parting the waters
of white foam–flooded minds.

But these nights we were all Black.
My father danced the Uncle Willie,
turning his feet in
then splaying them out.
Country.

And I wish he would again.
Nobody thought it strange,
The way we loved ourselves.

The Eiffel Tower

My father brought the Eiffel Tower   (Beautiful . . . !)
home to us in that sun-drenched southern city
across the Atlantic where once ships skimmed the surface
carrying cargoes of us,
headed home with his treasure
over the coast
into our home
in Mississippi.

Then
up north to the South
Side of Chicago.
In this house he placed the Eiffel Tower
where we dreamed of Paris
for he had seen the City of Lights
and lived to restore it
with his dark American presence.
He hung the Eiffel Tower
on the wall in the front room
and it became a part of us,
the bronze carving, foot high, a plaque—
                    narrow-peaked, six inches wide at base,
a map of the world's magnificence
we would see.

Then one day
my sister Rose asked, "What happened
to the Eiffel Tower?"

I didn't know enough to say,

Who conducted
such cruel theft of beauty
while we slept?

Hero-House

1. Yellow paint on brush.
   Black body leaning in wind.
   Mustached man. Father.

2. House yellow singing.
   Perched on rough earth perfectly.
   The air clear poison.

3. Man moves down ladder.
   Chest heaving, gasping for breath,
   Asthma fells hero.

4. Party in sun house.
   A sign of life on concrete.
   Welcome sung in songs.

5. Brown Black painter paints.
   Yellow house becomes white house.
   Our dignity space.

6. Eyesore on Front Street,
   Calls from white house to White House
   Junk car gone same day.

7. Garbage-piled alley.
   Hero wrestles garbage man.
   Hero in handcuffs.

8. Hero piano.
   Song rises, knocks against air.
   He makes a way strong.

9. He plants his eggplants.
   Grows an impure fruit of heart.
   Withdraws in shadows.

10. Builds Delta for us.
    Eleven tiny rooms wait.
    He comes back. White hair.

11. Hero hard to breathe.
    They move him. A bed of greens.
    Where he goes we love.

12. Spirit-catcher house.
    Every good-bye ain't gone.
    Hero shut-eye sleeps.

One of the Guys

He came to the front door.
I could see the wind move past him.
A rumpled collector.
After cans for a price.

He said,
"I knew your daddy.
Used to work with him
At the post office.
Used to work with Jack."

My eyes opened wide.
He smiled at my surprise. Madaddy called Jack!
Laughed a little. He knew my father
Was George to me.
I knew George and Sonny Man.

Jack was handsome and tough.
And better than all the fellas.

Jack was young. One of the guys.

I gave the man some cans.
And thanked him for the gift.

A Portion of the Story

Stockyard trucks rumbled
Up Wentworth Avenue
Across Garfield Boulevard
Down toward the slaughterhouses.
Cows, hogs—they called them livestock,
Penned, crashing in the truck.
We could smell hairy nostril-opening death
In the city that never wept.

Across from us
Bulldozers knocked out buildings
Like a prizefighter knocks out teeth.
For the longest time, unholy ground was all that was left.
Our side of the street stood stunned, in the city that never wept.

Then rabbits came
And snakes into the open field.
We played and dreamed of open spaces, caught rabbits there.
When someone broke into the cage and stole the rabbits
We were bereft
In the city that never slept.

They dug out a hole
In the heart of the city—
A cavern covering half our street. They poured in concrete.
They made the Dan Ryan Expressway.

Cars can go by night and day, day and night, where noise keeps
Coming in this city that never sleeps.

Decades. The slow rumble of time.
Chicago should have been used to it.
Blank houses and emptied lots, more people poured out.
A pounding out of losses until we were deaf. Then the thieves
And body counts of children in this city that never weeps.

We cannot record the empty parts of ourselves
Where memories never were
But were meant to be.
We toss and turn but cannot sleep.
Our eyes burn in this city that cannot bear to weep.

After the Killing

And you—
Have you ever known anyone
Who was murdered?

Timothy, shouting up the stairs
Through the mail slot,
Young and true Black male.

Darnell, hustling hard,
Work-dust on his hands,
Trying to do better than he had.

Billy, with his cousin-grin,
Uninvited, but welcome
To the Thanksgiving table.

The Quiet boy stabbed
The Joyful boy, served
His time quietly, got released to die quietly by
Someone else's hands.

And Joyce,
With the pretty smile
And sweet girl ways
Smothered
By her husband.

Little Loretta on Lasalle Street
Eyewitnessed murder, elephant-
Gunned down, her small bones . . .

Al and Duke, father and son,
Cleaning drugs from a building,
Doing the right, right thing,
Their smiles to break the heart.

I've watched souls rise,
Smoke signals signifying
Disaster here, seasoning the earth.

And you—
Have you known someone
Who died by another's hand?

Love in High Places

(in memory of Michael Jackson, 1958–2009)

Way up high
On the third-floor porch
Of the tenement next door

The country girl from Alabama
Would hold her eighteen-month-old

Over the worn porch railing
Like an expensive magic carpet
She was shooing the dust from

Swing high
Front to back
Side to side

Never letting go
Holding on for dear life

Terror and delight
Bright in her eyes

Loss and escape from it,
A smile on her face.

A country girl
In control of fate
And forces of the world.

When the superstar,
Face schooled to exquisite features,

Dangled his child
Out the window
In a foreign land

I knew he was
Country

Country
Peculiar
    Floods
    One lost glove
    Everybody crowded in one bed
    Too kind to strangers
    The impulse to give
Can't take it away

And you could not
Take the country
Out of him.

Didn't he hold on to that dear life
In love and would-be loss?

The body dangling
Swinging high

Against the world.

The Wisdom of Ghosts

The ghost butcher slices roast beef.
In the window pink chickens with rings
Carved in their feet.
Behind the counter, hams
Like the buttocks of big women.
The ghost butcher slices hams too,
Handles them tenderly
The way a man handles a woman
He loves.

The ghost cleaners is heady with steam
From the just-pressed garments—
Black men's suits with seats that hint a shape
And women's dresses and skirts.
They launder shirts in the waters
Of memory, starch strength.
There is no such thing as regret
Or guilty buyer's remorse.

The ghost pharmacist mixes his medicine,
Pours elixirs into bottles, counts pills
And capsules the doctor who stirs cough syrup
On State Street orders, both of them
Black men.

So much Black-owned, not all,
In this Negro neighborhood, a safety zone.

Everything moved from our moment.

But the ghosts stayed here, stay in our corner.
That is how I know the way things are supposed to be.
That is why I am telling you before I am a ghost too.

After Ablution

Living as a daughter
In this old dove-white house
I'd wash in warm water
Showering from a spout.

Through the window sunlight
Would pour like liquid salt
And wash over me in bright
Aura like Sweet Shoppe malts.

The windows were open and air
Danced in, caressing me.
Unaware of the stare
Of a man I could not see.

I spread perfumed lotion
Over my rich brown skin:
And with love potion
I drank myself in.

I loved those moments' freedom
Like a Gilead balm
Something for me, not them,
I felt an unburdened calm.

As I dressed for the day
I looked up and saw
A man there, legs spread way
Apart as if to gun draw.

Face aflame, I snapped
The blind down and slammed
The window hard. Then I racked
My brain. Was I a ham

He's wanted to hotly hold
Or a plum he's wanted to suck
And bite as the juice flowed
All over his tongue's luck?

Bellwether

She sits at the kitchen table and looks right
Out the kitchen window at the tree moving,
Branches, leaves moving. That's how she knows
What kind of day it is. The tree tells wind,
Rain, still heat, smothering snow. She will miss
The tree. How else to know the weather
Without watching TV or stepping outdoors
On the back porch her husband enclosed
But never finished making a real room.

She can do without the new apartment
She doesn't own, her son and his wife own.
She owns this house; over all its memories
She presides as mother necessity, inventing
A way out of roadblocks and detours, obstacles
In a city that practices hope and deception,
Stumbling and dance steps.

She used to look out that kitchen window
Right at the gray stone church with its high spire
Until it became an abandoned eyesore
And she prayed for it to be torn down.
It's a parking lot now, a clear space
With a few buses that belong to a smaller
Church she doesn't believe in—they don't

Treat you like Christians. They're white settlers
And we're savages they've come to save
With turkeys, ham, and tent revival music that knocks
Against the afternoon and evening.

The settlers called the police when her grandson parked
His car in that big, empty lot; said he was breaking in.
The police came like lightning, striking, handcuffed him,
Lean and clean-cut athlete. He showed ID, told them
About her and how she lives in the house she owns
And has owned for over half a century. They let him go.
He went inside and told her. Then he went to bed.
Trembling with troubles. The way a tree does at certain times.

Blizzard, 2011

Thunder snow swirling heavy.
Lightning wicked, bright
Through white wave on wave.

Inside we are two women
Permanent as the snow—
Aged mother, middle-aged daughter.
Lights gasp. We flicker. Afraid.

In this house as children
When the lights were out,
We loved to name the states
And their capitals by candlelight.

We named the countries
And their capitals—
And conquered the world.

Tonight if the lights go out
I will name the many names for God
My heart cries out.

The House on Wentworth Avenue

In this moment
a sweetness.
Mama sleeping
on the sofa. Near
eighty-nine.
The Black judge
judging
on TV.
I have begun
to say good-bye
to this house,
this apartment,
upper rooms,
we ran through
like streetcar
lines
making noise,
leaving our midnight
warring roomers
behind.

The Memory Borrower

for my brothers and sisters

I am the memory borrower, brothers and sisters.
I will keep you safe and sacred. I am a keeper.

I can take up where you left off.

Margie put her face down in the water
And came up gasping. I didn't tell
Her a thing because she was two
And hardheaded as a doorknob
That won't turn. Margaret with the eyes
So black they like night pearls
Pasted on pieces of white paper.
Singing, her voice is
Heaven scent.

Debra couldn't see much even behind
Glasses thick as Moon Pies, her
Eyes so beautiful hidden all those
Years, big as moons with ink spilled
In circles. She was always so little,
Food ignored her and didn't settle in,
Even peanut butter she ate with
Her fingers out of the jar, standing
With the refrigerator door wide
Open. In her last year she came home from

That revival around the corner the
City Church gave and she had
The sweetest smile. It was so sweet
I made fun of her being saved. And
She smiled some more. She died
Soon after. I never knew what

Jesus promised her in exchange
For her days. Fifty is young.
Don't you think? Especially when
You love someone.

Betty was always one to throw down
The bottle and make the shards
Pop up and glint on the
Sidewalk. She decorated the scene
of the fight Sharon finished. Sharon
was the finisher. Betty gave me a memory
I didn't have to borrow.
Betty is a bottle holding this
Fight in her like a burning liquor.
She is very fine and crisp in the throat.

Sharon got slapped for letting somebody
Cut her beautiful head fulla hair. Madaddy
Liked his daughters with their crowns of royalty.
He sure did slap her. Hard. Her hair was thick
And tough as she was. It was
The most beautiful. As an Afro
It was a crest (and Betty's too was eloquently Black.
Margaret. Debra. Cousin-Sister Billie Rae). I can see
Them now: Afros, miniskirts, and windowpane
Stockings. Sharon went to the projects with the church choir, singing
Christmas carols and the people tossed eggs at them,
O, Come All Ye Faithful.

Rose is not a flower, but an herb,
Rosemary. And that is for memory.
In our tiny room with bunk beds I searched
Her eyes for new contacts lost already.
Rolled way back in the balls of her eyes.
"There they are!"
"Don't tell Mama," she whispered to me.
She loves to give me stories—write this, write that—
Then take them back. She calls Aunt Emma Shorty

Because she is Shorty before the boys in the hood
Called all women and children Shorties, so they could
Feel taller and better about everything.
Rose ironed and changed the altar cloths every Saturday
For Sunday morning. Rose and Helen. You would have
Thought she'd have grown up and been a nun
With a black habit that cut corners and a white bib
To catch the crumbs and stains of prayers, then
A trim business suit looking like a lawyer for Jesus's law.
She married instead. Husband and two boys her mission,
Her cause, and the world was made flesh
And she dwelt in it, going out to heal and change.
Quick as a whip, with Jesus on her lips.

Delores chose the vocation of our father,
A garden for a dream, a place to be
Herself without reproach.
After she went down to the harbor and dated
The Africans when she was a teen, then the
Dependable Marine, she jumped the color line,
A husband we whispered about, then got used to,
His people were so nice, even if they were white,
They were good. She was widowed. Quietly.
Delores's two boys climbed out
The window on knotted sheets, fleet and curious.

She took to growing things, knowing the names
Of plants and flowers, feeding birds,
Living among Republicans.

Who knows when Cousin Willie Mae
Arrived. Queen of the South Side
Daughter Billie Rae not far
Behind flamboyant Willie,
Both of them fishing for
A better life. Living on the first floor,
Flashing west to Iowa.

Tip-Top, Wonder Bread, Silvercup,
Wanzer on Milk Is Like Sterling on Silver.
Milk and bread welcomed us to a land
Of milk and honey, a neighborhood prosperous
And well fed with essentials. Honey music flowed
Out into the street, covered us colored double-strong.
The smell of bread hung in the air, danced
Just above our heads with the songs.
Prentiss lifted milk crates and became a man
With money in his pockets, a stern pride in his jawbone.
Would not be taken down by wrong. Fought back
Older George, scooped mountains of ice cream on cones,
Sold stories and stocked shelves with memory at the Black-

Owned drugstore. Became a legend. Who left the City and came back when
        a Black man was Pharoah
And called for him. Both brothers fathers and husbands
And sons.
Tip-Top, Wonder Bread, Silvercup, the aromas of bread
Suffused the neighborhood, Wanzer on Milk is Like
Sterling on Silver, a brand of excellence, naming the space
We prospered in, filling us up with memories to survive

What wanted to break our bones, our traveling legs,
Embracing arms, our backbones that refuse to snap
Under the pressure of impregnable loss and dear
And inherited hope.

Vacant Lot

I wonder what came of that big-leaft tree.
My brothers smoked monkey cigars that grew.
It was a good place to dream who I'd be.
They raised me on that block with Black bills due.

The tree of heaven stank to high heaven.
I used to stand by the window and lean.
I would send my voice to rise like leaven.
I wondered sweet about all I would mean.

All that is gone now, even that old house.
In that place remains the two tall old trees.
My mother ran a clothesline, shorts, shirt, blouse.
What rises to sun is crowds of wild weeds.

An ache runs through me as I ride by there.
No one would ever guess leaves we still bear.

Frappé Toast

for Dr. Ann E. Smith

Here's to the streetlights, necks like steel giraffes.
Here's to the slow walks to the library on Saturday mornings.
Here's to the tiny lightning of fireflies worn as ornaments by cruel young girls.
Here's to the watermelon man in the alley, the milkman, the egg man, the
      Insurance man always at the door, bringing and asking in return.

Here's to the women in tight skirts wearing gold hoop earrings.
Here's to the street where the Holy Ghost danced above our heads
      And holy water was the sweat of our fathers' and mothers' brows.
Here's to the teas of spring where women wore variegated pastels
      The same sweet colors as their crepe paper table covers and ginger ale
      And sherbet frappé and competed for the best table design and
      Sweets and eats. And whoever lost one year prayed to Jesus
      To win the next.
Here's to the record shop and the music that opened like a fan
      And wound through the neighborhood cooling
      Our tempers, and easing the threats of predators
      "Darling, You Send Me," "Baby, It's You," "A Change
      Is Gonna Come" the slow dragging wind
      Carrying us along . . .
Here's to who we became, the ones who remember
      And believe that we can survive the storm
      Of bullets and disbelief if we hold on
      To who we are.
Here's to the ones who survived the waves
      And the whips and the pulling of teeth
      And forced entry and taught us how
      To survive and laugh at the ones
      Who hurt us, then tried to be us.
Here's to you and me and the ones gone to dust
      Who dwell in us and above us and around us
      Loving us.

Sacred Heart: A Triptych

1. 1948

Mama descending the church
Steps, baby in white
In hand. Mama head wrapped
In white, Mississippi. Baby
Rose in swaddling clothes.
Coming out Sacred
Heart.

2. 1984

Me. A swelter.
Middle of Missouri.
The tree-lined street
Interrupted by bitter bark.
"Aunt Jemima!"
Me. Turning,
Fanning, harsh, blind heat.
Ready to turn his cheek.

No kiss of peace.
Jesus, Sacred
Heart on a skewer.

3. 2010

Brown praise girls sway.
The Delta spring. Mississippi.
White. Blouses come out
Of sashes. Air. Waves. Dancers,
Drum, organ

Heartbeat
Sacred. Sepia People of God.
Heart. I
Was born to believe.

O, Mama,
Never leave me alone
Be a glimpse in the corner
Of my eye
On the other side
Of the tear duct O,
Mama,
Sit in the chair you always
Sat in and watch me
Half sleeping, waking
To see you watching me
Watching over me
Mama
Never leave me
Alone
I cannot live alone
Without remembering
You making me
Strong.
The world is hard
With danger.
The earth is not
Dependable.
O, Mama, I am your child.
I always was.

The Flowering Bamboo

Bamboos rarely bloom. Some have blossoms only once every
30 years. Then all the bamboos in the area may bloom at the same
time. Only the parts near the top of the main stem bear blossoms.
The plants usually die after they bloom. New plants grow from
the seeds, which look like rice kernels.

—*World Book Encyclopedia*, 1982

I have not seen, but I have
Heard enough to know
The miracle—

The flowering bamboo
Blossoms
     In its own time
     Thirty years or a century.
Answers
     Its own free will.
A light from the other side
Of the blackness
That holds us to the world.
Is here among us, above.
Our eyes scrutinize zealously
And we wonder—
The reasons.

My mother walks through the door.
Her beige-clay face
Beneath a straw hat. In
A dress that runs over an hourglass.
The peace and sweetness of her face

In her mother's face. Her mother is not dead
Yet.
My cousin lays rows of spiraled
Hair around my head,
An intricate field.
Blossoming black limbs twisted dancing
In ornaments. Blossoming complex necessity,
Cornrows over my wondering brain. Dreaming.

This afternoon has lasted since before
Forever. My mother bends over the deep river
Of my face, to lay a drifting kiss on my cheek
Where scarifications would be in another place
Written into dark water. Her mother has not died
Yet and I have not been broken.

Centuries inside of centuries inside of centuries ago
Something larger than a star, something
To whom star is bright grain of anything,
Something,
A tremendous bright All,
Breathed in and out
In awesome fire-flower full of magnets
And the thin petals of light   luminous
Lovely and awful
Give embrace to everything earth.

A night's worth of loving,
Without interruption
A blue lotus of longing
Ravenous to be.

      The umbrella bamboo of her face
      My mother
      Blossoming into
      Her mother
      Blossoming into
      Me.

My father has not died.
Her eyes forgive me for sins I need not
Be. Only Love.   Luminous the day
Breathing in. Breathing out.   Continuous.

Her eyes a tangible light, pulse, from the long side of
Blackness.
Centuries inside of centuries ago.

This continuous
Blossoming, spontaneous,
Ordered.
The strength of the embrace
That holds us to the simple
Benevolent earth
Not floating against the points of stars
Centuries
And centuries and centuries from here.

In the trembling now
In this decade and day in millennium
Why the light
From the side beyond the side beyond the side
From centuries of blackness
Light that holds together the great embrace
Of gravity arrives on
Page three of the daily news
And
The bamboo blossoms
Obscure as the births and deaths
Of Black persons and nations
In the back of the paper.

What meanings unfold? What meanings of resilience and strength?
And what would burst first full of knowing:

My brain: My heart? Or just my mouth? Assembling these signs
In poem
When what is wanted is flowering free memory flowering
Will and world flowering
Flowering and flowering, dream,
Flowering.

2009–2017

Providence

for Rev. David A. Jones

Life was eternal on that Black block.
On the corner stood the steeple of our church.
The taste of life lingers like grape gum.
I braved the streetcar-lined avenue for the store.
I was an invincible six-year-old girl.
The only thing above me was huge bright sun.

In the sky it beat down from heaven, sun
Spreading over every crevice of the block.
I thought I lived at the center, just a girl,
Catholic altar at the corner, and next door Baptist church.
I snuck and dodged across the street to the store.
Secreted in careful wrapper was the grape gum.

I was dizzy with the taste of grape bubble gum.
Over me the dazzling shine of the sun,
Behind me the riches, wonders of the store.
Around me the marvelous terrain of the block
On the corner the solace of my own church.
I took off running like a rocket-girl.

I was near midway the busy street, just a little biddy girl,
Crazy with fear and mouth full of grape gum,
I would see down the block the wide-open Saintified church,
If I had not been near blind from sun.
I was a child who belonged to the block,
Racing through traffic running from the store.

A car stopped short of me as I ran from the store.
The driver must have cursed the foolish little girl
Crossing the street in the middle of the block.
What would he have said about grape gum?
I stood still and so did the sun.
One God was watching over me from each church.

There was providence from each and every church.
There was plenty in each and every store.
There was a generosity in the people of the sun.
This is what I remember from that day as a girl.
When I almost died for a wad of grape bubble gum.
In the middle of the wide avenue on my Black block.

I am that block, and I am each church.
I am more than gum under big boots, and I am a memory store.
I was a Black girl, now I am a woman of the sun.

II. Wishbone Wish

The City Where Men Are Mended
And Women Are Made Whole

(An African-Americanized Folktale)

For Mothers
and Mothers of the Spirit
For my mother—
Angeline Virginia
Robinson Jackson,
The Good Mother.
Love never dies.

The Thread Unwinds

Some causes are worse than others.
You never know until they come to pass.
My story comes from a mystery school.
Everything cannot be explained.
Animals talk and walk and do human deeds.
Humans are animals too.
The blue roof is alive and speaks clouds and sensitivities.
Sunflowers grow tall as men on stilts on mountaintops
And lean toward the sun.
Rotund melons curve back to earth. Round
With their own progeny.
Pregnant, a pause
Is in the air
And so the story begins
To unwind
On the thread of a girl's voice.

A Beloved Girl Begins

I believe in today, spread out like green free
Gardens that just grow on their own.
My age-mates and I searched and played
By a Great Tree with a big, open belly.

We danced and sang as we picked sweet
Herbs for our mothers. Under a sun that hugged
Like a father, heavy and kind,
The light from his eyes.

It began to rain in swift sheets and we jumped
Inside the belly of the baobab tree.

And the devil, mischief maker chief,
Closed the belly of the African tree,
A cruel joke against the safety
We found there.

The rain traveled away from us
For it was traveling rain,
As the grandmothers say,
Different from traveling mercies
Nowhere in sight.

The devil laid down his devilish,
Lewd law—each girl must give up
Her necklace and dress
Before she could be free
Of the belly of the tree.

I would not give up my dress.
Stayed inside the belly of the African tree
The devil had sealed against escape.

While other girls ran away home
Nude, stripped of their tongues
As they squealed away and shrieked.
They panted my story to my mother.

My mother handed me down food
For days. I answered her voice
Alone in the dark. Stretched out my hand
To receive the plate of yams
And string beans, taut as cello strings.
The barbecued goat, she fed me strength.
Playing for the time I could climb out
Without her hand out.

The hyena, crazy with ambitious hunger,
Listened to the exchange between a mother
And a trapped daughter. Hyena studied
My mother's tender voice. Practiced
Like a pianist trying to get to Carnegie
Hall. Once he called
In the pseudo-voice I would not answer.
Twice, he called
In the quasi-voice I would not answer.

Hot, angry, I spurned his lowered, gloved
Hand.

The hyena laughed his coarse laugh,
Like everything was hysterically funny.
Wily.

He made the Blacksmith a gift he couldn't refuse
To alter his voice that hyena might deceive.
In return Blacksmith would receive a lift
To his spirits, a living by your leave.

The Blacksmith, a deft surgeon, worked
To construct a voice of sweetness and comfort.

Have you ever known a hyena to keep
A promise? To Blacksmith or lovely girl?
In my mother's voice he called, the price steep,
Steep.

"Reach out your hand and mother will unfurl
A feast of astronomical proportions
And good taste. Under the stars a safe world."
Hungry, I didn't notice the contortions

In the familiar voice. So reached for home
And received a beast who devoured me slow.
My mother, returning, discovered my bones.
She gathered me up in her tears, said, "We must go—

We must go to the city where men are men
And women women and breathe joy to life,
Back into your bones, so little, sweet skin.
No time to weep or grieve, the teeth like knives
That took you."

A Mother Muses

This is no fairy tale where I find
the hyena who ate her and slit
him open with a knife and she
leaps out whole and beaming
in a halo of light. He has
digested her without thought
and shit her out. He builds from her
cells, snout and nails. Teeth.

I have to begin again where she left
off. Pick up her bones. And place
them in a basket woven by women,
shake loose the dust from my feet,
and follow my road to the city
where men are mended and
daughters become again.

I ask the Wind the way to the city
where humans are mended and restored.
The Wind whirled and gasped with a great pity.

"Walking you will learn the way as you ask."

A dead daughter is dumb
dumb as dirt. Without solace,
plain as water.
Her beauty is lost.
Her winsome ways gone,
belong to Memory.
So Memory guides this mother
to the city in which she will be
re-created.

Not a day goes by when I do not
consider her eye-smiles and slim
thighs, up-slanted mouth and breasts
that rise. The memory of her
eggs me on, a quick step of anguish,
then funereal bereavement.

I never made my bed hard,
someone made it for me.
I get up often.
Make water.
Try to catch sleep.
I only catch the echo of my daughter's
wail.
Where was I when he tricked her
with the sound of my voice
the birds told me about?

I comb my hair, burn it, so the birds
do not fly me into madness.

Who can get through life
without committing a crime?
Which secret sin is mine,
the cause of this?

Ah,
remembrances surge to the surface
like dead fish
that stink.

It is my fault.
The fault is mine.

Since the moment
of conception
this feeling
—constant—
that catastrophe
will come. A wild
bloom blossoming
in my belly
along with her,
and after a trail of blood,
bright as a Nobel scientist.

Now this devilish bloom
grown-up
overwhelms
until I am blind
and peek through
its leaves
to see
where I must go.

Destitution

Not to hell and back
but a way station.
A workplace, a paradise
sanatorium,
a soul-spa, to work things out.
Turn grief, desperate as a fish bone in the throat
to a new daughter the same as the old,
no improvements necessary, restore
flesh to bone, organs, what resides in the hyena
belly, the same make, meat,
tender as the rims around a mother's eyes
red-raw from crying.

Goodness to Its Own Reward

And what do you get for it but a pile of bones?

A good woman goes to work every day
in the killing fields,
lies down on the killing floor
and *takes* it
like a good woman should. She lets out a holler
that slices the moon into wedges of pie.

She been the best she could
and what's she got to show for it?

A mirror of waters wiped clean of her image,
tears for a tricked offspring
trickled into the earth.

And she has to take it.
But she talks back.

As I Walk I Sing

Miss Bones,
     Ms. Bones,
          I said.
Do you love the Lord?

Shiver, shiver, and shake.
Daughter, Miss Bones,
I sang.
Do you really want to be
Back in the flesh?
Shiver, shiver, and shake.
Daughter, Miss Bones,
I said.
Do you long to feel my mother-touch?
Skin to skin, in a fierce Mama-hug?
Don't it make you tremble
To think of all you're
Missing?

I tremble. I tremble.
I tremble. Oh, Lord.
My darling girl,
I tremble for you.

God don't like ugly.

And He ain't too fond of pretty.

Is what this world is made of.
But it sure is pretty as my child
the way the trees stand alone
like the cheese in a child's song.
And do they all go back home?

To the earth.
To blue heaven, wide open
as the Conqueror's eyes.
Everywhere above, blue eye
where used to be soft berries' stain,
the spirit of crushed blue flowers.

Some people who could fly
flew back from the whip
and the shackle
to tell the story
of kidnap-no-ransom,
high hell-ships, all weeping
for fields, all enduring
until they flew.

Do I go back home
with Miss Boney MaRoney
or with my wishbone
mended
And come true?

Is this the breeding ground for bitterness?

Is this the breeding ground for bitterness?
My loss is so great—I cannot bear it.
Is this the time for toughening unrest?

My daughter is my hope and my true best.
I birthed her from my blood, fed her my teat.
Is this the breeding ground for bitterness?

Is my sorrow different from the rest?
Preachers say we are born tween piss and shit.
Is this the time for toughening unrest?

When joy lingered in me it was a guest.
The hyena stole it from me by teeth and wit.
Is this the breeding ground for bitterness?

Those girls who gave up virtue were no less.
My daughter too stubborn to take life's bit.
Is this the time for toughening unrest?

Three little birds in a tree sing

You can't cure everything.
You can't cure everything.

Pausing to eliminate, I wipe
myself with leaves. Why would
my gaze catch a tiny spider
scrambling like hot eggs in the sun-
light, looking for a hiding place
but there is none? And
the fact that I have seen
what was hidden by the rock
must be, must be, a sign
of immeasurable good luck.
My basket has never left
my head.

The Dead Speak

Yet

The Dead bedevil me.
They show me their still faces.
One writes me a note, "I do
Not like to be alone."
Others say, "We are waiting
For you." I dream.
I search for her.
I do not see my daughter's face.

What is the difference
between a bad neighborhood,
thug-lions loping and lurking,
and a rich one
of elephants ambling, showing off
ivory and ass.

It's all the same
when you are numb
to all
but one end,
one end justified:

a girl's life.
Means—what a mother must do.

This grief
protection against annihilation.

Number the flowers.

Colors.
Number the trees.
Number the spiders.
Numb.

Sumptuous Meals

A nightmare lasts a day,
a week or two or three
or more. Time
shuffles like a deck of cards.

Sumptuous meals
offered her
a sweet deal.

She came upon succulent
gumbo,
the Black Folks' kind,
okra roux.
The recipe
passed from Mother
To me and you.

She said,
"O food,
help me on the road
to the City Where Men Are Mended."
Then the gumbo, good eatin',
said, "Taste and see
the deliciousness of me."
But she answered back,
"I have no appetite.
I don't wish to eat you
now."

So the delicious gumbo said,
"When you have gone
a certain distance,
take the road on the right hand
and leave the left."

She traveled through
thick thicket and shadow,
lean road and brazen sun.
Another food
spread before her—yams,
candied sweets,
She shook her heavy head,
No.

She refused. Instead said,
"Show me the road
to the City Where Men Are Mended."
"Taste and see the sumptuousness of me,"
the yams, candied sweets proposed.
The mother shut her lips closed.
Her eyes welled open.
And the yams said, "I am
pleased." And the candied
sweets said, "How sweet the path.
When you have gone a certain distance,
take the road on the right,
and leave the left behind."

Her throat dry,
she took one sip
from her gourd
and let it drip,
trickle like a tear,
rain in her throat
with the unspoken
holler, hoarse cry.

"I can't even stop
for a cool drink of water
or my daughter will be
lost again and then again."
Irrational as a leaf
And brittle with grief.

A side of barbecued beef, luxuriating
in mambo sauce
suddenly beside her.
She repeated her entreaty, "O meat!
Show me the road
to the City Where Men Are Mended."

"Taste and see,"
the hot, sizzling barbecued beef
proffered itself. "Are you sure
you will not suck on sweet beef bones
and lick tasty mambo sauce from your delicate
digits?"
The anguished mother said, "I have no
appetite. I do not wish to devour."
So the barbecued beef ribs said,

"When you have gone a certain distance,
take the road on the right hand
and leave the left.
Since you will not stay to eat and run,
be gone to that city.
Travel hard and travel fast."
And so
she did.
She did.
And gone.

Upon reflection
in a clear pool
with quick, flickering fish
like bits of lightning
across my cheeks
momentary
scarifications.
I see my daughter's face
like my own.

A passerby thinks I am someone else.
This face.
African model #99,
molded across continents,
pretty,
prettier,
prettiest.
I appear
always mistaken for myself,
my daughter.

My husband is at work or War.
And I come to
the Garden
alone.

Knock, knock.

Who's there?
A girl who is bones
rattling, murmuring
in a basket woven by women.

Knock, knock.
A joke
Fate played on a good girl.
Where is the justice in this?

Three little birds in a tree sing

You can't cure everything.
You can't cure everything.

Being a good mother I was once
a good daughter who had to be
invited to eat. I lose interest
in food, only the sustenance
of my daughter's devoured
smile opens me to the
sunlight in the road that
ends in my shadow. I
do not tarry over all the
dishes that call to me, then
give me directions. Eat
nothing, then rush. Her
holy bones in a basket I
carry on my head heavy
with heartache. Oh, my pain
is interminable. I do not speak
a mumbling word.

Going Straight on the Right

The Good are ridiculed.
That's the way of the whirl.
She looked neither left
nor right, only straight
ahead.

Beside her trees laughed.
Bushes burned
profanely. So she prayed
her way through the periphery of terror,
       the random report of guns,
       smoke and fire,
       drive-bys of fly-by-night
       destiny.
       A countryside laid waste
       with Slim sickness.
       Thin, ravaged
women howling on the edges, hot
threaded like needles
with exquisite pain.

The birds in a tree tweeted to her

You can't cure everything.
You can't cure everything.

I keep on going, going to the right.

I keep on going, going to the right.
Daylight wheeling, spinning into deep night.

I heard of a place where trouble is solved.
I said, I heard of a place where trouble is solved.
Got to keep going, Lord, I can't lose my resolve.

       I keep
To the right.
       And there is no
       ease.

A peculiar loneliness
in keeping faith.

A stony road to trod.

"Did you think you were special?"
      a witch rustles in the trees.
"Did you think trouble don't last always?"

Which evil disturbs my journey?
I keep
to the right.

      In the distance
      I glimpse
      A shimmering, shimmering,
      an opal angel singing,
      "Ain't you glad trouble don't last
           Always?"

A New Sky

Once the sky was just above our heads
And you could reach up and touch sky.
Anyone could grab, eat until well fed.
The sky was sweet and low, not very high.

Then greedy people took too much of plum.
They squandered sky, took one bite and littered.
The sky wept, a cold rain, angry and glum.
The rain fell stinging, so very bittered.

Then the sky all plum and tender did rise.
It lifted past heads of the tallest men.
The people looked up in wonder, surprise.
They reached but could not touch sweet sky or wind.

The sky in this country is near the earth.
It is balmy here, not far from new birth.

Her arrival was in disquiet although the welcome was warm.
      Her hair standing all over her head.
      She was unkempt, disheveled,
        distraught, distressed.
A foot-soldier who has seen many battles.
And this,
the greatest.

At last,
she lay her burden down.

"I feel better,
so much better,
since I laid my burden down."

Welcome

A metropolis. This side
of heaven.

Plenty good room.
Animals ambled the grassy avenues.

Fruit trees abound, spread out wide,
reach high, dip low with bounty
dropping down,
strewn about the fertile ground.

There is a blue river
in which all bathe,
swift-moving to cleanse
and drink from.

"Brothers and Sisters,"
the Big Bull sang out.
"Welcome!"
His bellow belling forth like iron
and gold.
Calling her into the City
Where Men Are Mended and Women
Are Made Whole.

In the morning

given a task by the Archbishop—
I do the right thing without thinking of it.
Only an ear out for pertinent gossip
among the blessed, not salivating, salacious.
I rest and mind the protected beasts, the cautious cattle,
contemplative as cloistered nuns.
I feed them treasures   from a precious tree.
Fruit, fat and ripe.
I eat the bitter, hard, and mean
leftovers from the feast of the dumbest beasts.
I am
fine with it.
Fine with it
all.
I'll do anything.
Sacrifice anything.
For my future.
My lovely future.

What the little bird said

You can't cure everything.
You can't cure everything.
You can't cure everything.
The bird sent this thread down on the breeze.
You can't cure everything.

But I must.
I do the work I must do.
Shoveling doo, if I have to.

After Work

Well pleased
To see the cattle sleepy, satiated,
A woman weak with weariness, little fed,
With dirty work hands, at dusk,
The Archbishop Bull bellowed,

"This woman has a good heart.
Mend her daughter
Well."

She went to sleep

She went to sleep
humming a lullabye
to Baby Girl Sweet.
Wishbones. Wishbones. Wish.

Glimmering sparks I saw

In a half-sleep of peace
So sweet I did not understand.
I glimpsed
The descent of animal-angels, shining shapes.
Hulking as boulders,
lithe as leaves,
at wonder-work
over the basket of beloved bones
now out of my grasp,
relinquished to peace
to piece her again like a quilt of a nubile queen.

Oh, the blue river water, pounded red berries
they poured, clean,
blessed
to become her blood of my blood.
And her organs—
heart, kidneys, lights,
bladder, liver, and all
her insides.
"Praise be,"
I murmur in my sleep.

Praise be
the human being
that is being.
Becoming.

"Alive!"
"Alive!" the animal-
angels echo
the numinous, awe-
some All.

And my daughter
sputters and breathes
as I awaken
fully,
still astonished at the mystery,
the miracle of mending,
welding, weaving,
breathing.
Oh!

Oh, magical Imagination of animals
to re-create a girl
cell by cell by cell
until
she bursts a basket
and unfolds whole,
bone connected to bone,
sealed by flesh and sinew
and coursed by blood.

Oh, miracle Imagination
to make a daughter whole
a young woman
who has been
through it all.
Lovely, lovely, lovely
she returns,
reborn.

"Alive!"
"Alive!" The animal-
angels echo
the numinous, awe-
some.

And my daughter
sputters and breathes
as I awaken
fully,
still astonished at the mystery,
the miracle of welding,
mending, weaving,
breathing.
Oh!

Caress

With calloused hand
I caress
her plump rump,
her strict spine.

She is perfectly perfect.
And she is mine.

God is God and always will be

God.
A God of Mercy
and Mystery.

Amen.

So mother and daughter danced down the road
toward home.
Their footwork dazzling.
Their hips swaying, buttocks tight as melons.
Their heads on right, humble and joyous
and grateful.

A daughter, Happiness.
A mother, Sojourner.

Beauty is in the eye of the beholder.

So is Envy.

Upon their return to their village home,
A circle of women gazed and praised
Perfect Happiness.
They called tough Sojourner a good mother,
Kind and true, persistent as Elmer's Glue.

Another wife,
Another mother, raged inside.

You can't
put such Envy in a cage.
It bends bars.
It must be satisfied.

Motive Is Everything

Motive is everything.
Every morning the heart-
Muscle moved to its envy-engine.
She squatted in the shadows.
Above her a great gray cloud
Passed over the sun.
Behind her the big tree
Where trouble had been conceived
That led to wondrous events of an original mother
Who followed her heart and reclaimed it.

Another mother squatted in the shadows.
A woman who would have been
Beautiful,
If she had been beautiful. All
Long limbs, an arrogant turn
Of head. She lifted her chin
To sniff herself. A wild perfume.
Her victory on the Wind.

She squatted, leaned on her haunches.
And concocted a plot.

A Girl's Folly

Silly girl to come running so happily
    when her jealous mother
        called her by name.

Such a sweet girl,
Dark as a plum.
Grown freely in neglect.
Naturally good.
She came running like a little rabbit
When her mother called.
A girl
all bouncing and skipping,
like a lindy-hop
a dance of bliss, jerks and lifts
when War ended
and Peace was declared.
Kisses in the street.
Such a girl.

The Act

The women kept a huge mortar
and pestle in the center of the village
to grind great amounts of nourishing grain.
It stood like a large stone teacup
with no handle, a stone grinder poised inside.

The plotting mother commanded
the obedient, quick girl to climb
into the huge mortar to scoop up
some millet for her.

Eager to please, the limber girl twitched
her nose and curled her soft lips in a smile,
and climbed in.

It was murder by mother. Murder in
the first degree. Premeditated. Studied
evil murder.

Mortar and pestle she ground her guileless child
to white bone, red blood, and brown gruel
of cartilage, mucus, muscle, and brain matter.

She shrieked and grunted with each pounding,
"Fix her. Fix her. City. City. City of celebrity."

What She Said as She Was Grinding Her Up

A voice like electric shocks—
Gangsta muscle in each pounding

Bitch, I told you to sit down. *Bitch*,
I'm tired of you. *Bitch*, you stupid.
Bitch, you lazy. *Bitch*, you act like
You crazy. *Bitch*, you get on my last nerves.
Bitch, you ain't worth nothing. *Bitch*,
Pull your dress down. *Bitch*, don't
Bring me no babies. *Bitch, bitch*
Bitch. I will fix you. *Bitch*, I will
Fix you better. *Bitch*, better!

A girl-mouth, stretched jagged-wide in horror.
Smashed-in lips, teeth.
Then no lips, no teeth, no mouth.

A daughter's bones remember

a mother who never went to PTA meetings, who never
cooked dinners of greens and chicken and peppers,
instead fed cereal out of half melted plastic bowls
that were left on the hot stove. A mother who never
crooned a lulling lullaby or tested the temperature
of milk from a bottle's nipple, but plopped out a teat
while she puffed a cigarette, or jammed a cold bottle
in an infant's fist. A mother who left diapers on so long
a daughter's skin was raw when she was a baby,
and now her skin was thin as the Wind wound round
remembering bones swirling in a soup of blood and gruel.

Musings

A terrible mother—
She lumbered along, sweating
With the weight of her exertion
Now eased with the weight
Of the one she would berate
Upon her stylish head
Her relaxed hair so slippery
The basket almost slipped off.
She was sleek and slick
And graceless as a well-fed
Snake,

The cold eyes
Of a beauty contest judge.
"If only she hadna been
So ugly.
Things would've been
different.

"Everybody's not privy to my growing-up
Story.
My life was a struggle of stumbling
Blocks.
Why shouldn't I live on Easy
Street?
Beautiful as can be to rake in money
For me?

"Everybody knows
Beauty attracts Money.
Money attracts More Money.
More Money makes the World
Go Round."

A bird overhead tweeted to her

You can't cure everything.
You can't cure everything.

She moved in command

She moved in command.
Marshaling the birds to disperse
Before her. They sped like feathers on speed.
Her destiny was her destination.
She was in complete control.
Her daughter's destiny was hers to hold.

She slept like an elongated
Snake baby by night.
Strutted under her basket
By day.
Time raced to be rid of her.
Time quick like the ghost
Of a hare, or a rabbit-girl.
Sumptuous meals
Offered themselves to her
Like hot virgin men.
She ate everything that spoke to her.

"Show me the way
To the City Where Men Are Mended."
She came upon gumbo,
The Black Folks' kind.
The gumbo was simmerin'.

"Taste and see the deliciousness of me,"
The gumbo said.
She said,
"I believe I will." She said,

"You don't have to invite me
to greaze,"
and gobbled up
            the entire meal.

The meal replenished itself
and sent her on the left.

"Take this road on the left,"
it said. "And go on."

She traveled through
a clear path,
the sunny side of a wide
road.
Another food spread
before her—yams,
candied sweets
cooking in an earthen pot.

Without a thought
she accepted the offer to eat them.
"Taste and see," the succulent dish said
when she asked the way to
the City Where Men Are Mended.
"I believe I will. You don't have to
ask me to greaze," she said
with her greedy self.
Having gorged
like a fat rat she said,
"Show me the road."

The sweet potatoes, yams
filled up again and sent her
on her way. "Take this road
on the left."

So she did.
And came to a well.
"Well, well." she said,
and drank to her heart's delight
from a wooden bucket
she sent down and up.

Next she met a side of beef
barbecuing itself in the sun.
She slathered it in hot red
sauce and bit without being
offered. "Show me the road,"
she spoke through a full mouth.

"Suck on me please,"
the beef said after the fact.
Then it offered sweet bones
and tangy sauce which that witch sucked
and licked.
Then the barbecued beef
as dry bones clattered,
"When you have gone a certain distance
take the road on the left, and leave
the right.
Be off to the city,
well fed as you are.
No longer hungry
for anything.

"Travel as you will.
Travel as you might."

And so
she was off.

Party Time

Time knows no tedium for a woman without conscience. She
treads easily. Bones and muck in a basket on her untroubled head.
She was distracted by a commotion, bells and whistles. She hid
to look. The elephant was throwing a party in his grassy home.
Everybody was invited but the monkey, didn't know how to act right.
The monkey asked the lion to take him along, didn't know
the elephant said to the lion, "Get that monkey out of here!"
The monkey told the lion, "You the king of the jungle." The monkey's
business, safe under the lion's roar. The elephant pulled the monkey to the
side, stepped on him, *Kerplat!* Then the elephant looked at the lion and said,
"You next!" The lion looked at the monkey and said, "You're on your own." The
mother did not wait to be spotted, she inched away out of her hiding place. She
didn't want a footprint to cover her face. "I thought this would be my pity
party." She whined. "I am a mother who just lost her daughter. I thought this
would be my pity party." Then she picked up her daughter bones, her stepping
stones to glory.

As she strutted she imagined

what they would say.
They would call her

The Great Mother overlooking the earth.
They would carve her
a plaque out of the rotund stump of a tree

Mother of the Year.
They would give her a trophy of a golden
antelope, naming her in its elegance.

Their voices sang in her head.
Her daughter would be as beautiful
as sunshine on water.

Now bones and muck swirling, cracking above her.
She began to do a sassy cakewalk.
What would the bones say if they could talk?

"Mother, what have you done?"

She turned a deaf ear
to the world's weeping.

Dead bodies falling
left and left.

With dead eyes blank as eggs,
eyes that once were startled.

Slaughtered—in wars
on streets, in alleys, prisons.

She passed the Market of the Dead,
crowded and bustling with haints
and lingering souls, swiftly moving
or slow like shimmering clouds.

But no one called her name.
No one remembered her.
But they knew
her kind.

A bird overhead tweeted to her

You can't cure everything.
You can't cure everything.

The Way It Went

The copy-cat mother approached
translucent Truth
bathing in a deep pool.
Truth's clothing
a pile
beside the water.

Opportunistic as certain diseases
that Lie gathered up the clothes
of Truth and slid into them,
a raiment of grace
and modest maternity.

Outside the city gates
a crowd began to gather like bees
humming and swarming to usher in
the eloquently attired Lie
like a new queen bee.

She let loose a flood.
Tears of a grieving mother,
False as plastic teeth
Standing in a glass of water.

Truth rose out of the pool.
Floating head and shoulders above all others.
She glided to the side of the water.
Finding nothing
where once her raiment lay,
she stood—alone—
naked,

crushed to the earth,
yet rising
deep in her own spine.

Truth was silent
but not mute.
She watched the Lie
embraced by the city gates

amid confetti, ticker tape,
and a fall of red flower petals.

The Archbishop Bull

blinked
in the blazing sun,
gazed upon this second mother
with the remains of a slaughtered
daughter.
The bull belled forth.

She Kicked Back, Reclining

Given her task,
She took up residence
Under a heavy boughed tree. She sprawling slouchy.
Keeping weed in high esteem,
She smoked blunts one after one.
She gossiped with the coarsest birds and nibbled
On the fruit of the sacred.
The cattle rambled and ground grass
Hungry enough to cannibalize a cow.
Taking pity, she tossed them hard
As brass fruit.
She devoured the ripe bite by bite.
No thought of the bones of her issue,
She sighed
At the perfection of her pleasure.
The day went down in this way.

Cattle ambled in.
Seeing them, stoic and weak,
The Archbishop Bull decreed,

"This woman has an evil heart,
Mend her daughter
Amiss!"

A Hot Mess

A mess began.
Lumbering animal-angels descended.
Thrusting wildebeests of rage outlined
In spirit realm rhino, hippo, crafty crocodile
Craft crying vengeance.
Hot dust storms of devilment
Twisters twisting awhirl. Oh,
The cells miscreate and miscreate,
Make wrong and
Make wrong as a mother
Who spiked her life with stinginess and spite.

The cells miscreate
Make wrong
A fabric on a crooked Singer
Animal needle—teeth and eyes
Sewn askew and sewing
And so much gone
Made wrong.

High Noon

In the morning the fraudulent mother
Stretched out in satisfaction,
Sat up in anticipation,
Saw, burst basket.

Aghast
She gasped.

Call Her Consequence, Call Her Karma, Call Her on the Run

Call her on the run—
swifter than a whizzing bullet
the mother took off running, that dead-alive daughter
dead on her heels
a halving monstrosity
hobbling quick and dead
one
instead
of
two
eyes
nostrils
hips
arms
legs
feet
hands
half a smile
mouthing. "Mother, it is I."
one kidney
one lung
half a spleen
half a pancreas
a heart halved by horrible hurt.

The Curious Mother

Her wretched acts
Followed her, swallowing
Up the air behind her, dust and shadow.
All gobbled up
By the hobbling monstrosity.
Awful. Awful. Awful.

That half-a-thing followed her
All the way
Home.
Knock, knock, knocking
On her door.

"O, mother, I have come."
"O, miserable mother"
"O, merciless mother."
"I am yours for the keeping."

"You are not my daughter!"
The woman screamed. She tore
At her hair.

A Half-Girl

Here I hobble home to her
A half-girl
With half-heart
Half a mind
Half a brain.

Was it really my mother
Who pounded me up
With mortar and pestle
Down to bone and mush

Then carried me to the city
To be mended?
Carrying my bones, crying out her grief,
Caring not a fig for me.

Was it my mother who murdered
The woman I was meant to be?
Or someone else?

Here I hobble home to her
A half-girl
With one buttock
One budding breast
Half a belly
Half a navel pit
Half a mind to be done with this.

Who signed my name in blood?

In a universe created by a rival
Disguised as my mother,
Who took my life
And made it her own?

Yapping like a hyena
Or cooing like a dove,
Who mocked a mother's voice
And called me
Home?

She says I am not her daughter.
She is not my mother.
She never was.

Girls at Play

Look at the girls, lean or plump
And lovely, nubile and frisky, playing
As before all sorrow and re-creation.
A hobbling monstrosity among them,
Her mother's curse, no cure for her.
The girls take their clothes and
Shield her from curious eyes.
Her one eye open in immutable surprise.

Coda

Do not forget.
The devil was the cause of all this
The hyena doubled down.

Tortured, a mother proves
Her mettle.
Any woman does.
Any woman is a mother
              Of effect.
Any woman is a daughter.
Some women are mothers who are not mothers.

Yet
Every mother is a mixed bag of sweets, pleasantries, entreaties, and evil ways,
Elegant Truth and Difficult Consequences,
Whatever
Is in season

Yields plucked from the fields of destiny,
The orchards of fate.
Forgiveness reaps what repentance sows
Or forgiveness sows and reaps alone.
Grace breaks the rule of cause and result.

Nature is wily.
But, oh, nurture is worth the world.

III. Soul World

New poems
On various subjects
For True Friendship
Through the down years
And the bright years.

Snow Poems

I go with them
As they come.

The poems take
Their own shape.
Each one a snow
Flake.

They melt on my tongue.
They are so much sweet
Or so much grief,
A bliss beyond belief.

Now I'm making snow ice cream.
Add milk. Add sugar.
The way I did as a child.

When you eat it you will cry.

The Red Record

A Narrative of Lives Lost in Misdeeds Too Numerous to Fully Disclose

Homage to Ida B. Wells-Barnett, The Red Record *(1895)*

A Southern winter evening,
The dusk deepening,
The stars staggering across the deep sky,
He walked toward his father's house,
On the edge of manhood,
Chewing bright-colored candy,
Sipping sweet tea from a can,
Walking, the élan, the smooth
Rough edges of the hair
Hooded or out
Standing, simply
Being while Black.

The same state of flowers, same dark and stars,
Chilling in an SUV on his way to his father's house,
Loving living,
The gas station lit up with lights and loud sound,
The edge of manhood, his crew
Thrilling, the music in their veins,
The swag in the beat,

Pulsing with energy, pressing out
Into atmosphere,
Life, irrepressible
Being and Black.

The deep music of the skin, melodious,
Hurting the eyes of fearful men.
The movements, swigs of grace
Burning rage in the throats of angry men.
Smiles, bent, singular wing of angels torn by vicious men.

On the edge of manhood
Being while Black, poised magnificent.

Here lie incidents primed like a blue wall:

A giant of a Black man standing alone
On the New York sidewalk, accused of being
A misdemeanor by felonious men
Who rode him like a beast
Of burdens. They burdened him
Downpressed in a chokehold.
"I can't breathe." "I can't breathe." Eleven times.
They held his breath
Until it was not.

They looked in his face
And spoke to the absence
In the land of the living.

Walking in the middle of the Missouri street
On the yellow line, his swag
Owning the broad day. Nineteen
Like that. Feeling himself.
The cop pulled him over. Then
The story changes like a gambler's luck.
Witnesses say it was murder—
"Hands up, don't shoot." After he'd walked away.
"Hands up, don't shoot." Shots. Six.
Black young man broad body lay
Four hours in the middle of the Missouri street
In broad sunlight.

A daydreaming boy playing alone on a playground in Cleveland,
Toy gun in hand, on the playground.
Someone called, suspecting toy,
Cop car pulled up, two seconds, quick as nothing,
Boy falls from bullets, real police bullets,
Twelve years old,
Playing while Black.
His sister wept like Jesus wept
Over him. They tore her away,
Threw her in the squad car.
Weeping illegal while Black.

Early in Cali the Black young man,
How he partied on New Year's Eve.
On the train, an altercation
Near Fruitvale Station,
The cop shot him point
Blank.

In Phoenix he was running
From the OxyContin in his
Pocket, the marijuana
In the car, the jail time
For him, policeman
Wrestled him,
Shots to torso.
His nine-year-old daughter wrote,
"Why didn't you taze him?"

Nervous men jump at shadows.
Jittery men pull the trigger at their imagination.
Jealous men throw down the coat of many colors—black, sepia, tan, yellow, white.
Threatened men cannot serve and protect,
Uphold the peace.

I can't breathe.
In Cleveland
137 shots fired into a stopped car
That fled for an hour, police said,
They feared for themselves
From a gun, nonexistent.
Existed: a woman, a man,
137 shots,
Policeman on the hood of the car
Shot into the windshield over and over again.
How many bullets does it take
To take a man's, a woman's breath
Away?

In Baltimore, minor arrest, cuffs and ankle shackles.
They threw him in the paddy wagon
On his stomach, a rough ride, like
A sack of onions, body crying in layers
Spine broken, dying slowly.

Crashed his car in the Carolina night.
No help at neighbor's door. They
Called police at
His call for help.
He walked toward police,
Empty-handed as an infant, loose hands,
They shone everlasting light
On him. He ran
Toward the searchlight. Into the light.
They shot twelve times.
Handcuffed
His dying limbs
Afraid
Of the Resurrection
Of the Body.

In Cincinnati, Texas, Baltimore
In Ferguson, Missouri, Carolinas,
In Florida, New York, Cleveland, Ohio,
Chicago,
Magnificent, the lion-hearted people,
Have you seen the dignity?

Sometimes father, pride of pride,
Sometimes son, sometimes woman,
Sometimes daughter,
Sometimes a mane amazing.
Stopped in the act: being Black.

The eyes of the killer surprised.
"I did nothing wrong."
"I have a license."
"I have the right color." "I have a badge."
"I'm standing my ground."
The eyes of the killer surprised
By the spotlight,
Relieved by release,
License renewed.

The Red Record, a multiplication table
Of blood.

Someone said,
"She should have put the cigarette out."
And given up
Her last right to be herself
In her own car,
Driving where no law was broken
By smoking.

The officer told her to
Put it out.
He said, "I'll light you up."
(Like a lit cigarette
Then
Put you out.)
He dragged her out
Of her car.
He reached into her car
And pulled her out.
The long arm of the law
Against the law.
Shoved her onto the ground
And slammed her head down
Like a football
And he was making a touchdown,

In Chicago
He wandered down the center
Of the dark street,
Turned away
From police out of cars,
Sixteen shots,
Dust leapt up,
Sixteen shots in his jacket,
His body toppled.
And what of the girl
In a crowd caught
A bullet, Chicago.

In Minnesota
A Black woman with
Terrified eyes records
The murder of her man,
Her child watches
From back, the blood,
Final breath.

In the South
Police bear down on man
Hug and shoot.
The streets come alive
With outcry.

The cold wall, sea to sea shining,
Dutifully, yet hegemony stands
Without guilt, or shame or blame.
How to cleanse wrong when wrong
Is lifted up, acquitted?

I break the record. The names too
Multitudinous to list. I break
The record listing obliteration
Of Black presence, élan, beingness.
I cannot keep count.

No one hates police
Who come to the door
To settle the argument.
Nobody hates the cops
Who stop the robbers.
No one hates police
Who wrestle the murderer
With blood in his eyes.
No one shoots the sheriff
Who shields the woman
And girl and boy
From the rapist.
Nobody despises
The deputy who honors
The law and brings
An order that honors
The human heart and dignity
Of every man, woman, and child.
No one hates the policeman or
Woman who wants to go home

At night, kiss the wife
Or husband and the kids.
Watch the moon. See the sun.
Eat his gun. Or put on suit, shield, baton, and go on.
No one hates police
Who bring respect
Instead of blood on their hands.

Coda

Who can forgive
An American sin?
A church held saints who loved
Even the one who hated them.
As they prayed with eyes closed,
He gunned them down in the sanctuary.
A nation wept and the wicked winked
Through processed tears.
A flag came down
In a ceremony of grief and regret.
Yet the wicked proposed
The Confederacy to fly serenely
In parks so that animals
Might salute.
I'll tell you this truth.
We love everyone and thing God has made.
Yet the wicked, the evil, must work
For forgiveness
Even after we have, at last given it.

Changes

1

We danced double Dutch like spinning
Wheels and drew Sky Blue, we played
Obedient Captain May-I and rough
Red Rover on the clean, open street.
No one took us down.

Now shadows walk under sun.
Boys armed with unforgiveness and guns.
Take aim
Against ourselves.

2

She was sleeping in her own bed.
In her own room like a cocoon.
When a bullet found her.
You think one won't find you?
You think you'll float like
A butterfly?

3

Someone lured him to an alley.
They wanted to even
The score.
They took his life
Like a drink of water
To satisfy their thirst
For cold blood.
He was nine years old.

4

In a dumpster
His body burned
Like a match.
I don't suppose you know
How the story of our
Childhood changed.
Will you float like a butterfly?
Or rip the wings from one?

The Bandits of the Garden

Boko Haram,
Who wanted bitter where better was,
Dragging away the bright flowers
Of the unguarded garden,
Broke the birds of Paradise and scattered them
In the forest,
Trampled them.
Who fought for the virgins, stolen as concubines and wives
Reciting the Koran on command?
Who pressed the blooms between the pages of the ruined Holy Book?
Boko Haram
Could not bear such sounding beauty,
The untouchable light of hope, of girls.

Hand Fishing: Loving

You have
to grab the massive cat-
fish with your bare hands.
Grab by the insides of the
wide mouth, away
from its teeth, its gills.
It can kill you. Drag
you under. Cut you
until you bleed, if you
don't catch it just
the right way. I know.
I've had practice.
I've done it before.
Once or twice.
Call it what you will.
Noodl-ing, grappling,
Hand fishing.

Men are better at it
Than women. I don't know.
Men have bigger hands.

Love Plots

In secret spots in the heart of the country
Hot-hearted men are plotting.
They name themselves Christian
Warriors. Christ, their general.
Jesus wept.
The rest of us slept a deep sleep
While they collected weapons,
Doubling up on the Black President.

They come out of nowhere.
An ambush against reason.
Empty pockets places to fester messily.

The cruelest question is color.
The answer is in the blood.

My mother waits for eye
Surgery and the doctor is late.
She pries off her wedding ring,
Hands it over.
I laugh with my sister and try
Not to blink. Death is tricky.
We have to watch for it.

Where does it come from
Such love that causes my fingers
To tremble as I hide

The ring grandmother gave my mother
In the purse my dead sister's son gave her
for Christmas?

Jesus, you know the cause you are leader of.

On a Sun-Fire Street

What to do with this uninterrupted rage?
I am the one-armed
Black woman.
I am the short one-armed
Black woman.
Eight months pregnant.
Left, lone arm
Flailing.
Fighting someone twice her size
In the sun-fire streets.
A bully bullying, lying on me,
Stealing my time, my love, my self
Trying to take me from me.
What to do with this uninterrupted rage?
Can you picture me
Enough to see my soul
Shining
On the sun-fire street?
Fighting.
Cursing solid bricks
I throw at anyone hurting me, my love.
This one arm is might!
Is what I got to box with.
To aim the truth
Against thieves
What a one-armed
Black woman to do
When her world
Won't do
Right?

Between the devil and the deep blue sea

Drylongso: a man named Joe, Mr. Brown wrote to sing,
A woman, Caldonia, or Cleo like a queen who lost
What's left of her name,
Or something some mama made up
Or my mama passed down to me. Some men just got an initial.
Or a certain way they push the air around them
To make a name for themselves.

Drylongso: poised between the cruel elements,
And the deep blue heat of unloving law.

Drylongso: a throwback to who we used to be,
Who we dreamed when we dreamed as one drum.

Drylongso: lonely as all get out
Big as all outdoors, the disappointment piling up like snow.

Drylongso: This blue heat brings a blues that trembles
In the teeth, a wisdom wondering when will come
Replenishment, retribution

Too much to hope for, isn't it
After all this shit?

Why We Respect the Flag

Tough enough to be funeralized twice.
At my father's funeral in Greenville,
Mississippi,
We knew we had at last
Reached his resting place.
We'd burned up highway
After a solemn, lovely mass
In the City of the Wind,
Flag draped casket
While we rode,
He flew above us.
At the funeral in the Delta,
A southern cousin read his life
With his good deeds
With his starry eyes
And stripes on his back.
My mother loved all she remembered
And forgave the rest.
We felt complete at last
To take him from Cousin Bee's funeral home
To the cemetery.
We gathered round the gravesite.
My mother sat on the mourner's bench.
At last some uniformed representatives of the government
Took the red, white, and blue flag
And folded it.

Folded it,
Folded it,
Precisely,
And put America in my mother's hands.
Along with everything my father had done.

We stand with a hand over heart.
Or not,
Lock arms, raise fist,
Or kneel or genuflect
For what must be fixed because of it.
This flag

Retrieve the stars.
And take the stripes from our naked backs.

On the Edge: 2017–2018

Old men told us about the edge
Of the earth, where we fear the cliff
And the monster with the open mouth
Under it.
All of us here are bereft.

We've wrapped our sails
And folded fast our nets around all the quivering stars that were.
We've seen this time and again on
TV where every thing's so tiny we can believe in it.

The world's a strict ruler
That will slap your palm
If you disagree.

What happened when no one was the wiser?
The world turned out to see that it was flat after all.
We sat on the edge of it with our legs hanging down
Looking way into the predatory sky to watch one sun eat another one.
The terror above so great, some of us leapt
Off the side of the world.
Others fell into the terror below
And drowned inside a dream
Like tiny spiders in a demitasse of whiskey.
Strong drink that did not keep us warm
From the cold.
Outer space, I am told, is so cold you cannot think it.

All of us here are adrift, cut loose from gravity, floating.
In truth it hurts to think so we do not think of a world so round
What happened tomorrow will happen today.
Where no one is wiser.
And what stars we gathered in our nets long ago died.

The tiny man on TV lumbers smaller and smaller
And so do we.
Who are we?
What are we to do?

Emancipation Proclamation

Today I wrote
my Emancipation Proclamation
and kept it over my rib cage
where it remains
declaring me a free Black
Woman.

My pass
into a land
with no overseers.
And no drivers.

I no longer work from can't see
to can't see. Though I work
by lamplight
discerning
my rights—

life, liberty, health,
justice, honest pay,
my own name.

Today I wrote my Emancipation Proclamation.
I am on my own
With my own kind of kind.

No others may walk with me.

The UnMother

Homage to Gwendolyn Brooks, "The Mother" (1945)

Barrenness will not let you forget.
You remember the children you wanted you did not get.
The small, quick bodies who ran like scattered seeds.
The singers and musicians who never played their reeds.
You will never scold or whip
them, or shush a trembling lip.
You will never coat a thumb with hot sauce
Or tell monsters under the bed you're the boss.
You will never go out the door, longing for them
Already, returning to hold them with arms sure and steady.

I have loved them, the children of mothers,
fed them food of comfort and sugary sweets,
let them suck from bottles I warmed,
and burped them after they were replete.
But then I knew they were not mine
And never would they ever be.
Though they lay in my arms and slept
And ran to me when they came to sit on my knees.

If I deprived them of birth and names,
Their hollerings and their hand-games,
Their romances, and raps, and squabbles
And scowls, marriages, illness, and
deaths,
If I stole their only attempts at breath,
Believe that the crime was not solely mine.
He never came to father you, cure me kind
And tenderly.
And so you could not be.

Barrenness will bring regret.
I gave myself to other gifts.
But believe me
And this truest that I can recall.
I wanted you. I wanted you all.

Electric Blood

for Renee

West of the City, the birds sang like faint factory whistles.
Trees came to that town to hide
among houses like they were in witness protection.
Houses as neat and tight as the knots
on men's ties worn on Sunday after Saturday
night when blues reigned then packed up
and moved subdued to this suburb.

I was not much more than a girl when I met
the Bluesman's daughter. She, a little dark
angel, offered me her father's record,
which I refused. She didn't
have to give me anything for a smile
and a poem that I came to bring.
In that land of milk we were swirls of rich honey.

The blues took his daughter to the suburbs. If
you see her as a woman, tell her she was special
as a little girl, even though her father's name
was legendary. The blues was in her and my blood.
I'd already bought *Electric Mud*.

Tell her we have so much in common:
My father was the blues who never was
famous, and we never made it
out of the City.

Tell her she was always royalty,
never sequestered in anonymity.

Checkerboard: A Blues Lounge

for Christine

Because you are Black does not mean
you understand what it means to be quiet,
the night opening around you, above you,
holding you in the small noises

of slow distant cars and crickets you can hear
in the country, or yourself thinking
about your life and who you are and who
really loved you after all.

Because you are white does not mean
you are right about the best of the world
and what is due you and the dues you
paid without knowing what extra dues

were paid by others with knuckles bleeding
like yours. Sometimes Black people are white
like that and some white are Black
and quiet, good listeners,

heads tilted, listening to the click
of some traffic sign inside, a green light,
a yellow, a red, waiting for new signs and wonders
to arrive, quietly or loud.

Her Love in Autumn on the Church Bus

She considers when she was young and supple
as a spring flower bush,
blooms beginning to show.
She leans her head back on the cushion,

and remembers the shyness of her love.
How it was never spoken,
but sung through her eyes.
She kept her desire closed, barely open.
The way it was.

Now she shields her eyes
and rests her thickened body on the bus
cushion.
Every day is worrisome, working as the leaves
work color to remember.
The only wondrous thing is memory,
alternating with hope.

Does a woman get more
than one love
in her life?

Ask the bush.
See how it burns!

Black Girl Dreams of the Perfect Partner

Standing before TV in her tap shoes, she'd
see Bojangles man and Temple curl-girl.
Temple boll of cotton, candy, a pale confection,
tapping, dimpling the world. Bojangles, tree,
set free from American soil, raise roots, touch
them down light as leaves. Torso held precise-
ly.   And smile sudden sunlight flash through dark
branches.   In half-spin hands held light.   He
all weightless wonderful, bright heavy smile
hanging through history. He, in Hollywood costum-
ery, buckdancing on the dusty doorstep of the
backdoor welcomed in kitchen smells and bedsprings;
Blackgirl don't know how lovers dance behind closed doors.
He the world to her before TV new tap shoes on her
feet. He bootdance in diamond dust on the other
side of the world,   rise out of dark mines,   shake
diamonds off big shoes light as leaves like rain
off leaves,   the ease of him. Heavy, quick smile
hang through history on her girl's heart she wish
she bigger for her own wish.   She wish she open
the back door, be the woman in sunlight, on bed
springs she don't dream. She wish she dance once
once with Bojangles pick up diamonds with her teeth.
She talented Ten agile magic   floating with Mr.
Bojangles Robinson, elegant among ghosts in nineteen inches
of dream.

High John de Conqueror

In an antique magic shop on State Street
In a glass case there a High John
de Conqueror Root, tuber, testicular,
"Gonna mess with you." I put my young girl
Eyes on it and wondered about the power
Of a man to make a woman be still,
Dance, or speak in an unknown tongue
Of romance and *Please, please me,*
Ride me, till my back ain't got no bone.

I could see it all standing there,
Staring into the glass at the High John
de Conqueror Root of Dr. Feelgood
And the Heart-Breaker. My love life
Laid out under glass looking
At that root of all evil blues
And good goodness of life.
You really got a hold of me.
You really, really do. Will you conquer?
Or will you be true?

Sermon (Or, What the Black Woman Said to Herself)

I tell you
You tear-glazed star-starer
Eyes lifted above you
There's nothing there, but more of you—
You—
Breast of the Milky Way.

You are your own Drinking
Gourd
To ease your
Thirst.

You are never lost
In the company of heaven.

You are never lonely,
Knowing the sun
Will rise.

And your body believes
In dreams.

Swag

I am the woman who rode
The alligator to town.
Who tied his mouth shut with a string
Of pearls.

When the people came to see me cry—
I am the woman who tamed a tornado
And put out its eye.

The Coat

While crows perched in trees
and broke the cool air
with their callous calls,
I walked like a soldier
too good for my own good
wearing my moth-eaten coat.

But inside was a coat of many colors,
a kente cloth I wore
to keep me warm.
I promised all who would listen
I would share it
with multitudes
who would fit inside.
Its folds hold the old ones,
pockets cradle infants,
one and all wrapped
in the luxurious fabric.

This coat is less than the wings
of angels, shielding them,
but more than
what weather, foes, and the hawking
of crows
have stolen from me.

More Than Meat and Raiment

for Cornelia Spelman and Reginald Gibbons

Perhaps dream figures of fire and wind
Spirit-being gathered up in human being momentarily
More than flesh and flashy garments
More than supper and skin of many colors
More than meat and raiment.

Age, gender, race, hue, aristoi, data to discard
After when and why and wise—identity on earth, momentous momentarily
Who you are is who you are—a-blaze
Inside, a-bloom, a-risen, all the ages
You have ever been remember
All the stories you were ever told
All the stories you ever told
All the songs you ever heard sung
All the songs you could barely hum
All of these winding around inside you
Like a choir of remembrance.

Blood of heritage,   blood of spirit
Promise and delay,   clamoring
Stammering child, weeping woman,
Howling, crying man, talking baby,
Blood of heritage,   blood of spirit.

Injuries, slights, neglects, abandonments,
Assaults, bruises, all the hurts you have
Endured, survived and did not
But took inside, these are you
As much as the fire leaping up and out
And the wind spinning round, delight, and comfort, succor
And hilarity, a-trembling

Soul-piece, God-lamp, heart pumping red
Blooded blue blood true blood round
Bone of bones, bone of honor, bone of strength,
Backbone connected to the wise head bone connected
Through the body bones to bones all connected
More than themselves

All the feelings felt recur
Course through thoroughfares
Of thought, riding and gently
Twinkling like little lights, strung
Around, around through
Until the mind breaks with love
Or worrisome need, desire is a firework
Opening up this moment into a thousand thousands.

And then more than that or this
More than words or images
An invisible indelible indivisible
Infinite beyond age the numeral
Or gender the sex or wish or race
The wise or myth or class the money or
No money or manners or hue the grades
Of color or aristoi the steps above
Below more than concept or conceit,
Food and clothing, elusive as freedom-need and justice,
Belief or disbelief, the presence of awe,
And awesome, awful and discreet, replete
And contiguous, night and noon at once
And more than anything we can name now or then or
Once, more than meat and raiment, far far
More than.

And then there will be more for you.

Praise Dance

Rose paints a picture of a
Woman dancing to the choir
Music in French, Spanish,
Or English or African
Tongue.
This praise dance is
Impromptu
Yet perfect to
The songs of each mass.
Did she rehearse
In Côte d'Ivoire
Or heaven in her mind
Where no one can
Clip her wings
Or drag her out
Of the door
Away from
The eye of God?

Cumbaya: A Cry

Someone praying—someone
Praying, Lord.
A prayer in the hush-harbor, witness the whip,
A scar in the singing, stinging throats, tongues,
Flesh ripped and torn by thorns of cotton,
Tobacco leaves, sharp rice, grit, caned by cane,
We hewers of water, drawers of wood, carriers
Of dirges and sorrow songs, civilizations and burdens,
Others' leisure and profit and pleasure.

Sing a soul in a clearing, a song up
Rising, cumbaya, not a word for careless
Who never knew or forgot hurt secreted
From the tear-ducts, a message to God.
Who would not forsake. Cumbaya, Lord.
Remove this sorrow stone on my road.

The Dead

The Dead live in the house next door.
No wide yard divides the houses.
A white fence separates us from the Dead.
We lean over the fence to gossip.
"How's the weather?"
"Isn't the weather crazy?"
The Dead agree with everything we say.
Sometimes they disagree
And interrupt us in a dream.
Will Mama come visit today?
Will Sister come back to smile or deride?
Daddy is asking for what he needs.
Brother says, "Do not talk to the Dead. They want us to come
Over to their side of things. Soon."

But they are so happy to see us.
We go to sweet sleep.
In the morning they wake us
To live up to them.

Money Trees

In the yards of certain people
Money grows on trees—
Their boughs stretch out gracefully.
Splendid the dollar leaves.

Money trees—magnanimous to a few.

Ah, certain people recline
In the shade of bounteous trees
And do whatever they please:
Sip mint juleps, engage in gossip
Vulgar or discreet, devise designs
To cause their privileged trees
To prosper and whisper in the breeze.

Or
Like the winged of the air
And lilies of the field
Certain people neither sow
Nor spin
But spend their days
Raking leaves leisurely
From the money trees.

Or
The yard boys and girls
Rake the leaves
From the wonderful money trees.

We who live in stark sunshine
Burn from the glare of the sun,
Stand in treeless yards,
Sweating from our labors
Without benefit of kinder, gentler shade,
Dreaming of trees of money.
How green the dream
And the envy of certain people
Coveting all that dollar leaves confer.

How easily we forget
Crisp leaves fade and burn
In the fall.

We rouse ourselves from the dream
Of money trees. We do what we do.
Given branch to replant,
We swear to be generous to a fault,
Bestowing leaves in many hands.

We swear we will share
Even the smell
Of new money.

At the Movies at Bennington

Tonight I watched *I Walked with a Zombie*
In an auditorium in Vermont. White
Winter outside. White people all around me.
Some nice. I think. I missed

The call and response of Black
Folks, the art of talking back to the white
Black-and-white. I was happy for onscreen color
I could imagine in my people. The intricacies,

The human touches. But the anger rushed
To my throat. "Philip, who the hell is Inez Wallace, who
Wrote this?" I growled at the teacher. "They
Got some of the African religion right."
Forget the skull at the crossroads. The Hollywood
Choreography.

A gentle man, he said, "I don't know. A little bit
Of Jane Eyre in there." I could see
The noble nurse, the bitter husband.
His redemption, the mad-zombie wife.
The terror in the night.

The drunken brother, guided by voodoo,
Thrust the bronze arrow in the blond zombie.
Burdened by love, he walked into the sea.
While the bulb-eyed tall Black sentry stood
Watch for the gods.

Oh, the voice-over Black man had the last word
And blessed the conclusion and the union
Of the noble nurse and redeemed husband
While the corpses were carried in.

I walked out into New England snow,
Watching my own breath, bereft in history.
A line from the movie haunting me:
A rich cane-man's claim the coloreds weep when
A child is born and laugh when someone dies.
The legacy of slavery. You ever heard anything
That crazy in your life?

I consider the scenes that I love:
Dark men supping on the arrival ship while the sea shone.
In the night, the drumming in the background on the island.
The Black island musicians strumming and singing a taunting
Song in the square, mocking the owner. The pretty Black maid
And friends rejoicing around a new Black baby boy; they said

He would smile at a friend. He smiled at the noble nurse;
She pinned him. And toward the end, Black men went fishing
In the dark with pouches at their sides, spearing wide,
Big fish and lifting them out of the water like ghosts.

The next morning I dream in Technicolor.
On the cliffs Black islanders parade to the sea
With offerings of yellow and orange flowers. The Black voice-over
Spoke: *And the sea will love the Negro.*

Asylum Baby

She crawls crying across the concrete
Searching for something soft
Embrace, language above her
Hard not soft music tongue
Something soothing, diapered, crying
She scoots to the edge of cement
Floor she'll touch her tiny fingers as
Petals to the metal web she cannot name
She has no word for jail or cage or prison
Or labyrinth baby's breath trapped
Barely word for mama for papi, no words for
I want soft to hold me, me
No word for me.
No word for free.

Toward Bliss

for Robert and Anthony Lawson, and Matthew Jackson, who all survived

Limitless sorrow rooting in cities and towns, hamlets,
Sorrow trees and hedges of grief surround us,
Keep us in their gloom away from the sunlight
Of sweetest bliss. They call this "pandemic,"
Grim, relentless, full of spite against
The living. We fight to be free, well,
And tender. We fight to live, not hauling long distress.

Whichever would cheat us of breath
We resist; nations, peoples, the world
Rises up against whichever would keep us
From sweetest bliss and fulfillment.
We wear the masks that shield and hold
Us safe. We bare our arms
To bear arms in battle for life.
We stand discrete; are reluctant to touch until clear.
We wash our hands like Pontius Pilate, assiduously.
"What did we do to bring this plague?"
We murmur.

Each week the news concludes with
A stream of obituaries, notices of
Ordinary wondrous people who once
Lived lives where they were loved
Or not, but are missed and wished
Here with us; God, our ancestors give watch
And lend us strength to endure,
Prevail, so we go on and walk toward
The turn in the road ahead, the glimpse of
Sunlight past the shadows of sorrow trees,
Toward the promise of singing
In the distance, our songs of sweetest bliss,
And wisdom we have earned.

A Tale of a Comet

NEOWISE, July 2020

Just think—
The comet tonight won't be here
For another 7,000
Years. How long
Will its tail stand still
In the night sky?
To last a memory
Of a life.
And that any-named boy shot by
Another unremarked boy,
How long will his
Memory hang out
Under the streetlight?
Or the Black woman, lovely and beloved daughter,
In the dark, not much more than a girl,
Cozy beside her boyfriend/best friend
Shot dead
Out of her own bed, battering ram
At the door. How long
Will last the spark in the memory of her?
Or a cuffed Black man
With an intentional knee
On his neck
For nine minutes
While so many people cried out and watched
As if he a comet to appear again
In 7,000 years. Or the next
Day on the evening news.
And what of the rest
Of his flash across a lifetime
As son, brother, husband, father,
Kinsman, moving like a comet, big

In the sight, a life lived
In relativity, getting by, loving
Wherever, whomever he could.

Him, her
Just think
How love follows a person's life
For
7,000 years.

The Good News

for Senator Jacqueline Collins

Now we stuff the low-hanging fruit
Into our mouths.
And it is spiked, acidic
Our mouths bleed.
The news—infants and killing gasses, gun violence.
Presidents and prostitutes, police as assassins.
And what of the high-standing fruit
That shines in the light
That blinds?
We reach and reach again.
We dream the taste,
Sweet and true.
These fruit are hope.
We shake the tree, smashing the long-hung fruit that falls.
And the tall-held fruit, they fall at our feet
While we tread like sighted light
In a dance
Of first justice, then
Peace.
Mouths run sweet:
Justice. Justice. Peace.

The Surface of the Earth

for Sarah Odishoo

Hiding on the surface of the earth
Dark children concealed
From the ruptures of explosions.
Child-soldiers stolen from their play.
Smiles torn from their faces.
Weapons cradled; they are not cradled.
How to name the countries?
Border wars. Squalid squabbles,
Women ripped inside, birthing rape-babies
To squall untouched in the villages
To which they returned, discarded, ruined
Edifices of the spirit.

Astronauts floating like flowers on clear water
Can see the holes in the planet,
The wept waters, all of it,
Past. Present, would-be future
Forgotten, misbegotten.
Children pour out of schools
Like too much salt and pepper from a wound,
Dying in a school.
Salt in a world of salt water, human tear ducts.
Peppered tongues of screams.
Wars and rumors of wars.

Astronauts can see what we can be.
A calm presence. A great One-ness.
An articulate goodwill. A covenant of Saints,
All radiant, revealed.

A Gathering of Tulips

for Joyce Carol Thomas

The tulips, purple and yellow,
Gather on both sides of the door
Of the doctor who promises to give
My mother clear sight.

We are happy to see flowers
Stretching up, on elegant lines,
Opening their mouths
To sing us into spring for a moment.

Some of them, purple, are still closed
As people who keep secrets, like me,
And some of the yellow are opening
To receive new breath
So they can sing louder
And wake the dead.
I want to open my lips
and sing like these.

Two choirs of tulips gather and send up
A rousing gospel shout—*I never would have made it*
Through the blind nights of winter.
Now through this sign of flowers, upright, opening—
I got the Victory.
It is a promise I believe—
Soon and very soon everybody will see.
Everybody will sing.

Ida's Call to Action

for Carole A. Parks and the Ida B. Wells Legacy Project

"Eternal vigilance is the price of liberty."
And we must pay in tender of wakefulness
and action.
Must needs be not silent in the face
of monsters for
monstrous deeds make a man a monster,
and monsters walk and rule and legislate
among us, answering the call of the least
loving or wise, the most spiteful and venal.

Their world is arranged around color and
cash, gold and precious elements, and oil.
We must not forget the gush of oil
out of the earth like fierce black blood.
Who holds the earth's wealth holds the health
of all the children everywhere. Believe and know.

Monsters must be toppled or immobilized,
silent gnomes or odious ogres' licenses
revoked to ravage as they please. And
the number who hoist them up higher to
their monstrous heights awakened from
the sleep of their consciences and
moral dreams. Be propelled to angelic action
and deeds of virtue and brightened self-interest.

My legacy is thus—a womanhood on fire with seeing.
Hearts abloom bravely, a sisterhood set to battle
for right. Brothers beside us.
Are we of one accord?

For Our People

Homage to Margaret Walker, "For My People" (1942)

for our people everywhere singing
their gospels and their rap, their blues,
R&B, and their jazz, their soul and their neo soul, all great Black music,
scuffling, scrimping, struggling to get by,
for our people working as wage slaves,
in collars blue, white, and pink, doing the best
they can with what they have, hoping
it will not be taken away with a pink slip,
a sudden slip from a parapet, on cement
into disability or welfare, or not,
hustling to keep from being crushed
on the unemployment line

for our people
for the way of years sipping summer from a tall glass of ice water,
buttermilk and cornbread out of a mayonnaise jar,
years testing watermelon, cutting a plug of sweetness,
knocking on the round or oblong to listen to the taste,
for the excellence of young boys running like they stole something
but only owing themselves and the strength in their legs
and girls who could keep up before breasts held them back

for our people and red Kool-Aid days,
for smothered chicken and our cries smothered
in a world that did not adore us, but ignored us
or worse and ran us back on the other side of the viaduct
where we belonged, not in the wild world we could conquer
or excel in, given the gates opening and tools for redress

for our people everywhere
growing gardens on vacant lots, training roses
and black-eyed susans and perennials in front yards, raking

leaves and shoveling snow. scooping doo and picking up
litter, washing and ironing out the wrinkles of everyday existence

for our people
running with nowhere to go, watching
television and movies looking for ourselves, searching
books and the nooks and crannies of history
for a glimpse of what was waylaid, and what is to be,
in barbershops and beauty parlors and ice cream parlors
and the stone faces in funeral parlors, picking up children
from school from daycare, taking them to football, soccer,
baseball, tennis, basketball, volleyball, having a ball
at family reunions on Saturday nights

for our people who came in chains
tortured over turbulent waves, broken
hearted, and broken tongued, and broken magic,
broken bloodlines, strangled and whipped, distraught
and driven to the edge of the mind, and beyond
for our people leaping to the sea, feeding sharks and myths and cautionary
tales, surviving the journey to reach auction blocks

a prurient pedestal for deposed queens, and chieftains, villagers
humiliated, abused, raped, and riddled with misery into
exquisite survivals, changing vocabulary and clothes, changing
into sleek panthers and superheroes, making the world safe
for demonstrations of protest and affection, all beauty and love,
scapegoated, pilloried, denied the excellence we bring

for our people grasping for gadgets and genuflecting
to electric celebrity, worshipping trinkets and noisome
symbols that blink and itch the eyes, gaming and gambling
and laughing to keep from crying, and crying laughing,
cracking up and falling out, drinking suicide, and spilling milk
and blood, gunned down under lampposts, in playgrounds,
bloodied in drive-bys, in alleys, in living rooms, in bed sleeping

for our people bludgeoned by police and each other,
killed by presumptuous watchers, taxed for Black and driving while Black,
shot in the back, falsely convicted, sentenced to dwell alone, and
want to be redeemed, incarcerated in stone, tracked in department stores,
harassed, stalked in malls, and all the places people spend and sell,
our people selling loose squares, oils, socks and peanuts
on the corners of our desperate longing, for hair, for nails, for body
graffiti

for our people in the casinos, scheming in pennies from heaven
with one-armed pirates, dreaming in die and cards and dealers,
dreaming numbers and playing them till they hit,
for our people drowning in spirits, burning throats and pockets
losing it all, spoiling livers, lungs, and kidneys, hearts with too much,
each of us addicted to drugs of fashion, to ancient hurt,
choosing crabs in a barrel or lifting as we climb, each one teach one

for our people who do not belong to me but to all of us for we belong
to each other, must hold each other in heart and mind
for our people in the citadels of learning and the one-room schoolhouse,
in the storefronts of funeral-parlor fans and the cathedrals of painted windows
and arched ceilings that lend toward sky
for our people in the baptismal pool, in white robes on the edge of the river,
for our people, chanting and praying and hoping for a sweeter brew to sip
and savor

let a new earth arise
let justice pour like trembling rain and mercy prevail as plentiful fields
let our strength be matched by vulnerable honesty of heart
may resilience be our guide, for we will stumble and then will rise
more able having fallen, more beautiful having met each other
along the way as we lifted each other up, hero-people who go out of their way
for love, and stay on the way of goodness

let our people be the people who remember and believe that love is all our
    portions
all our currencies and all are one, each of us injured or exalted, betrayer or
    betrayed, muted
and declamatory, all one, each of us all of us, each a private star beloved in
    the universe,
each of us creature of burdens and singing angel merged as one, alive and
    moving upward
holding on and lifting this earth, our house, precious and precarious, and
    God be our witness
between this gravity and this grace, hold tight and fly